Highlights

Hidden Pictures

CHRISTMAS PUZZLES DELUXE

HIGHLIGHTS PRESS
Honesdale, Pennsylvania

baseball bat

envelope

rabbit

snail

fishing pole

magnifying glass

bat

ring

baseball

fish

2

scissors

mountains

glove

sailboat

ruler

Art by Josh Cleland

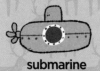
submarine

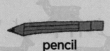
slice of pizza

pencil

toy top

wedge of cheese

button

3

Animals' Tree

The animals will love this Christmas treat! Can you find all the hidden objects?

candle

mushroom

peanut

spoon

crescent moon

ghost

chicken

slice of pizza

picture frame

feather

leaf

sock

whale

pencil

clamshell

fork

Art by Gary Mohrman

4

Which things in this picture are silly? It's up to you!

Art by Gary LaCoste

Six by Six

Each of these small scenes contains **6** hidden objects from the list below. Some objects are hidden in more than one scene. Can you find the **6** hidden objects in each scene?

Hidden Object List

The numbers tell you how many times each object is hidden.

bell (3)
boomerang (3)
button (4)
cane (4)
crescent moon (4)
crown (2)
fork (2)
heart (4)
ruler (3)
slice of cake (2)
tack (2)
worm (3)

BONUS
Two scenes contain the exact same set of hidden objects. Can you find that matching pair?

Art by Jannie Ho

Penguin Songs

Sing along with the penguin choir as you find the hidden objects.

sailboat

pennant

lollipop

envelope

screwdriver

strawberry

cupcake

comb

Art by Lorraine Dey

Trim the Tree

Art by Svetlana Larshina/GettyImages

Making Cookies

kite

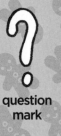

question mark

spool of thread

crescent moon

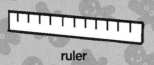

ruler

drum

crown

comb

seashell

Something smells delicious! Can you find all the hidden objects?

shuttlecock

test tube

top hat

flag

Art by Dana Regan

paddle

feather

tube of paint

crayon

Merry Music

Can you find at least **14** differences between these two pictures?

What do alpacas sing at Christmas?

Fa-la-la-la-la, la-la-llama.

What do sheep say to shepherds at Christmastime?

Season's bleatings!

Art by Josh Cleland

What is a librarian's favorite Christmas carol?

Silent Night

What did the beaver say to the Christmas tree?

Nice gnawing you!

spoon

pennant

sailboat

magnet

ladle

lighthouse

magnifying glass

saucepan

horn

fishhook

skateboard

eyeglasses

lampshade

14

boomerang

closed umbrella

toothbrush

hockey stick

ice-cream bar

rocket ship

Art by Kelly Kennedy

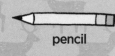

pencil

slice of pizza

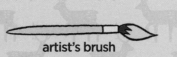

shovel

artist's brush

paint bucket

ring

Snow Day

There are **6** words (not pictures!) hidden in this scene.
Can you find BOOTS, CHILL, FROST, ICE, MITTENS, and SNOW?

Art by Kelly Kennedy

Say each tongue twister three times fast!

Silly snowmen make children smile.

No nose knows snow like a snowman's nose knows.

Shovel snow slowly.

Gingerbread House

What a festive gingerbread house!
Can you find all the hidden objects?

toothbrush

ring

teacup

candle

pencil

golf club

needle

spatula

nail

wishbone

spoon

snake

fishhook

handbell

tack

Art by R. Michael Palan

Can you find at least **15** differences between these two pictures?

Tic Tac Row

What do the sweaters in each row (horizontally, vertically, and diagonally) have in common?

Art by John Herzog

Who hides in the bakery at Christmas?

A mince spy

What kind of Christmas sweater does a pirate wear?

Arrr-gyle

19

Give this boy something to think. Then find the hidden cane, football, pencil, slice of pizza, and stamp.

Art by David Coulson

Jingle Bell Rock

Time to make some merry music!
Can you find all the hidden objects?

Art by David Helton

crown

sailboat

golf club

sock

necktie

screwdriver

pencil

chili pepper

leaf

wedge of lemon

seashell

puzzle piece

flowerpot

loaf of bread

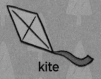
kite

21

pickle

stocking

snowman

holly

peppermint

mitten

snowflake

toy bag

musical note

reindeer

sled

bell

santa hat

ice skate

This street has been decorated . . . with hidden objects!
Can you find all the objects hidden in this photo?

Christmas tree

mug

teddy bear

star

piece of candy

candle

candy cane

string of lights

sleigh

wreath

Christmas tree ornament

gift

gingerbread cookie

Christmas Concert

spoon

travel mug

musical note

L square

horseshoe

envelope

crown

flashlight

magnifying glass

wedge of lemon

snake

slice of pizza

bell

Everyone loves the kids' performance. Can you find all the hidden objects?

leaf

sock

domino

pencil

baseball

boomerang

golf club

heart

bowling ball

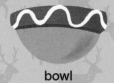
bowl

teacup

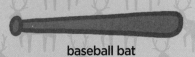
baseball bat

Art by Mitch Mortimer

27

Time to Party

Unwrap some gifts with these elves, then find all the hidden objects.

artist's brush

lamp

tack

hammer

beachball

domino

needle

lollipop

bird

book

candle

ladder

traffic cone

candy cane

pennant

pencil

pocket watch

slice of pie

butterfly

worm

toothbrush

ring

caterpillar

party hat

snake

heart

banana

sock

crown

snow cone

magnet

bell

leaf

Art by Diana Zourelias

Christmas Town

How does a polar bear decorate for Christmas?

With mistle-snow

What is another name for an artificial Christmas tree?

Faux fir

Each of these scenes contains 12 hidden objects, which are listed below. Find each object in one of the scenes, then cross it off the list.

Art by Chuck Dillon

ball	caterpillar	horseshoe	seal
banana	chicken	megaphone	shovel
bell	envelope	mop	slice of pie
boot	fish	penguin	stocking
candle	hammer	pitcher	squeegee
canoe	hockey stick	sailboat	toothbrush

hourglass

ballet slipper

Christmas light bulb

crayon

pinecone

snowflake

Aloha!

Build a sand-person, then find the hidden objects.

boot

glove

peapod

sailboat

feather

rabbit

Christmas Dance

ice-cream cone

boot

spoon

hairbrush

clothespin

nail

penguin

frog

bell

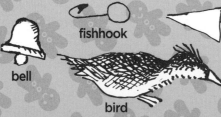

fishhook

arrow

bird

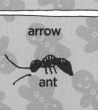

ant

roller skate

The animals have gathered for a Yuletide dance. Can you find all the hidden objects?

mitten

fish

strawberry

sailboat

toothbrush

key

three ducks

seal

saw

fork

shoe

Art by Valeri Gorbachev

Light Show

canoe

wedge of lime

pencil

crown

slice of pizza

paintbrush

button

spool of thread

horseshoe

shark

piece of popcorn

banana

funnel

toothbrush

bell

golf club

sock

hammer

puzzle piece

envelope

Art by Dave Klug

crayon

comb

needle

carrot

ruler

Night Skate

There are **6** words (not pictures!) hidden in this scene.
Can you find COOL, CUT, MAN, SEE, SNOW, and TELL?

Art by Jackie Stafford

Say each tongue twister three times fast!

Twila twirled twenty times.

I see icy ice skaters.

Skipper skated skillfully.

Let's Decorate

These friends are having fun decorating the tree.
Can you find all the hidden objects?

Art by Sally Springer

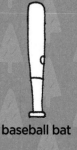
baseball bat

slice of cake

nail

hockey
stick

flag

ring

spoon

book

mitten

sailboat

banana

comb

pencil

musical
note

high-heeled
shoe

clothespin

envelope

hairbrush

mug

bowl

Tic Tac Row

What do the snow globes in each row (horizontally, vertically, and diagonally) have in common?

Art by Garry Colby

Double Birds

Art by Kevin Zimmer

How would you decorate gingerbread cookies? Decorate the cookies here.

Winter Journey

These animals have reached the North Pole!
Can you find all the hidden objects?

Art by Mark Corcoran

tent

ax

wishbone

scissors

ice-cream
cone

ghost

crown

lollipop

shoe

high-heeled shoe

tape dispenser

whale

toaster

firefighter's
helmet

45

Ornament Match

Every ornament in the picture has one that looks just like it. Can you find all **10** matching pairs?

Art by Chuck Galey

Snow Go!

Art by R. Michael Palan

Candy Canes

Can you find the apple, bell, cherries, fire hydrant, heart, ice skate, lobster, magnet, mitten, mug, necktie, scarf, sled, snowflake, and strawberry?

BONUS!
Find seven cardinals.

Letter Drop

Only **6** of the letters in the top line will work their way through this maze to land in the numbered squares at the bottom. When they get there, they will spell out the answer to the riddle.

A C H B E R A O R R L D E

1 2 3 4 5 6

What do you call a flamingo at the North Pole?

___ ___ ___ ___ ___ ___
1   2   3   4   5   6

Art by Jim Paillot

Night Flight

ladder

shoe

piece of popcorn

cookie

snow cone

heart

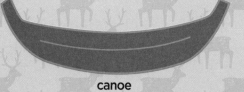

canoe

mitten

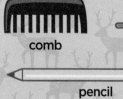

comb

needle

pencil

fishhook

bell

envelope

balloon

magnet

ice-cream bar

hockey stick

crown

football

ruler

sailboat

worm

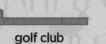
slice of pizza

golf club

Art by Gary LaCoste

51

Which things in this picture are silly? It's up to you!

Time for Cocoa

Grab yourself a treat, then find the hidden objects.

boot

candle

fishhook

hockey stick

mallet

hatchet

crown

banana

button

tack

needle

pennant

crescent moon

sock

drinking straw

Art by R. Michael Palan

Six by Six

Each of these small scenes contains **6** hidden objects from the list below. Some objects are hidden in more than one scene. Can you find the **6** hidden objects in each scene?

Hidden Object List

The numbers tell you how many times each object is hidden.

canoe (4)

comb (2)

cotton swab (3)

flashlight (3)

leaf (3)

lightning bolt (3)

lollipop (3)

mallet (4)

peanut (3)

pitcher (3)

popcorn (3)

waffle (2)

BONUS
Two scenes contain the exact same set of hidden objects. Can you find that matching pair?

Art by Brian Michael Weaver

55

Cocoa Contest

Who will win the contest?
See if you can find all the hidden objects.

slice of pie

magnifying glass

kite

pennant

saltshaker

horseshoe

key

flowerpot

necklace

banana

ring

nail

canoe

seashell

Art by David Helton

Give this girl something to say. Then find the hidden carrot, flower, spring, tennis ball, and worm.

Art by David Coulson

Christmas Dinner

chef's hat

flag

artist's brush

crayon

flashlight

bowling ball

banana

paper clip

yo-yo

chocolate chip

Time for a family feast! Can you find all the hidden objects?

golf club

wishbone

crescent moon

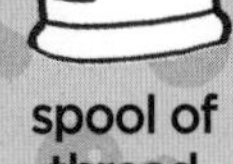

spool of thread

book

Art by Dana Regan

stamp

drinking straw

fork

toothbrush

We're Singing

Can you find at least **16** differences between these two pictures?

What is an elf's favorite singer?

Elf-is Presley

Where did the Pilgrims celebrate Christmas?

Jingle Bell Rock

Art by Julissa Mora

Who gets involved in the most holiday parties?

Christmas Carol

What is a Christmas tree's favorite Broadway musical?

My Fir Lady

ladle

ladder

kite

spatula

glove

piece of popcorn

comb

umbrella

caterpillar

spring

domino

ruler

lemon

Let's play a game while waiting for Santa. Can you find all the hidden objects?

Art by Peter Francis

nail

harmonica

safety pin

cane

boomerang

feather

sailboat

necktie

potato

scissors

heart

wristwatch

toothbrush

Santa's Workshop

The elves are hard at work making toys.
Can you find all the hidden objects?

egg

pennant

open book

bird

domino

ring

raindrop

needle

paddle

candle

shoe

funnel

ruler

crayon

nail

fish

Art by Gary Mohrman

64

Sledding Fun

There are **6** words (not pictures!) hidden in this scene. Can you find CHILL, COLD, FROST, ICE, SLED, and TOBOGGAN?

Art by Kelly Kennedy

Say each tongue twister three times fast!

See the skinny ski slope?

Sally's sled always slips sideways.

Tyler took a turn on Trevor's toboggan.

Who brings cats presents on Christmas?

Santa Paws

Why did the Christmas cookie go to the doctor?

She felt crumby

Each of these scenes contains 12 hidden objects, which are listed below. Find each object in one of the scenes, then cross it off the list.

ball
banana
bow
button
carrot
clothes hanger

envelope
fish
fork
glove
handbag
horseshoe

ladder
mushroom
slice of pizza
snail
sock
spoon

tennis ball
toothbrush
trumpet
umbrella
watermelon
worm

Art by Paula Bossio

Can you hide this candy cane in your own Hidden Pictures drawing?

Snow-friend

That's a tall snowman!
Can you find all the hidden objects?

Art by Catherine Copeland

ruler

ax

snail

nail

drumstick

coin · beehive · heart

eyeglasses

comb

snake · castle · fried egg

Ornament Search

Can you find the bell, button, candy cane, Christmas tree, Elf's hat, gingerbread cookie, holly, mitten, pencil, peppermint, reindeer, ring, rocking horse, slice of pie, snowman, and stocking?

Art by Rich Powell

Reindeer Games

Can you help Herbie find which reindeer or pair of reindeer is tied to each lead?

'Gator Skaters

ruler

fish

sunglasses

three-leaf clover

horseshoe

slice of pizza

canoe

skateboard

egg

bone

bell

Art by Kelly Kennedy

candy cane

funnel

teacup

ladle

cactus

coffeepot

snake

slice of pie

slice of bread

apple

ice-cream bar

Ice Sculptures

Art by Chuck Dillon

Rabbits' Christmas

Gather around the Christmas tree and find all the hidden objects.

Art by Valeri Gorbachev

light bulb

telephone reciever

hairbrush

crane

scissors

ice-cream cone

spoon

fishhook

fish

vase

ring

lamp

ant

roller skate

Festive Trees

1 Draw a large half circle on a piece of cardstock or posterboard. Cut it out.

2 Roll and tape the half circle together to make a cone.

3 Trim the bottom edge of the cone so that it stands up straight.

4 Use glitter, glue, pompoms, straws and chenille sticks to decorate the cone.

Peppermint Melt-Aways

1. Adult: Preheat the oven to 250°F. Line baking sheets with foil. Combine 8 room-temperature egg whites, ½ teaspoon of cream of tartar, and ¼ teaspoon of salt. Beat with an electric mixer until foamy.

2. In a separate bowl, mix together 1 cup of granulated sugar and 2 cups of powdered sugar.

3. Adult: Add the sugar a little at a time to the eggs as you continue to beat them. Add 1 teaspoon of vanilla extract and 1 teaspoon of peppermint extract. Beat for about 10 minutes.

4. Swirl in a few drops of food coloring. Spoon dollops onto the baking sheets.

5. Adult: Bake for 1 hour until the cookies are cream-colored. Turn the oven off. Leave them inside overnight without opening the door.

Before You Begin
Wash your hands.

You Need
* 8 egg whites
* ½ teaspoon cream of tartar
* ¼ teaspoon salt
* 1 cup granulated sugar
* 2 cups powdered sugar
* 1 teaspoon vanilla extract
* 1 teaspoon peppermint extract
* Food coloring

TRY THIS!
Dip the cookies into melted chocolate and decorate with sprinkles or colored sugar.

CONFETTI Ornament

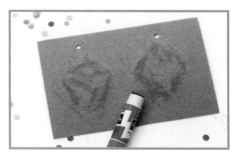

1 Use a hole punch to make confetti. Or, cut thin strips of paper into small pieces.

2 Draw your favorite shape on cardstock. Cover the shape with glue.

3 Sprinkle confetti on top of the cardstock.

4 Cut out your shape.

5 Add a ribbon loop.

Twinkle-Light Lineup

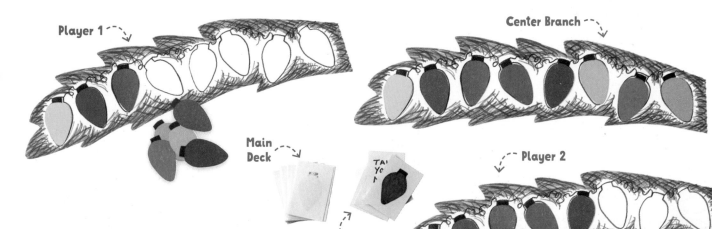

Player 1

Center Branch

Main Deck

Discard Pile

Player 2

1. Cut out a light bulb shape from poster board. Use it as a template to draw a row of eight bulbs on poster board. Draw a branch around the row, and cut it out. Make two more branches. Use markers to color the edges green.

2. Use the bulb template to cut out three bulbs from each of eight colors of paper.

3. Cut out 34 cards from poster board. Draw light bulbs on 32 of them. Color the bulbs (or glue on paper ones) to match the bulb colors from step 2. Make four cards of each color. Write "Take your next color" on the remaining two cards

To Play

Give each player a branch and 8 light bulbs (one of each color). Place another branch in the center, with 8 light bulbs on it. Players will fill their own branches, from left to right, with bulbs in the same color order as the center branch. Shuffle the cards, and place the stack facedown. Take turns drawing cards, and place a bulb on your branch only if the card shows the next color you need. Discard after each turn. If you draw "Take your next color," place the next color you need on the branch. Reshuffle and use the discard pile as needed. The first player to fill his or her branch of lights wins.

Holiday CHEER Mix

You Need
* Dried cranberries
* Toasted oat cereal
* Shelled pistachios
* Pretzel sticks
* White chocolate chips
* Cinnamon
* Nutmeg

Before You Begin Wash your hands.

1 Pour the first five ingredients into a bowl. Add two dashes of each spice. Mix gently.

2 To give as a Christmas or Hanukkah gift: Scoop the cheer mix into a container. Add a ribbon and gift tag.

Gift-Wrap Wreath

You Need
* Wrapping paper
* Styrofoam ring or cardboard ring
* Bows or ribbons

1. Cut leftover wrapping paper into strips. Wrap them around a Styrofoam ring or a cardboard ring. Tape the strips in place.

2. Decorate the wreath with leftover bows or ribbons. Hang the wreath on a door.

PEPPERMINT
Treat Box

You Need
- ★ Felt
- ★ Round container with lid
- ★ Treats
- ★ Plastic wrap or celophane
- ★ Ribbon

1 Use felt to decorate a round container and its lid. Fill the container with treats.

2 Wrap the container in plastic wrap or cellophane. Tie the ends with ribbon.

Snowman Builder

You Need

* ★ Styrofoam balls
* ★ Jar
* ★ Markers
* ★ Felt
* ★ Glue
* ★ Pompoms or mini foam balls
* ★ Ribbon
* ★ Butter knife
* ★ Plastic jar

1 Cut off the bottom of three Styrofoam balls. Cut off the top of two of them. Make sure they can fit, stacked, in a plastic jar.

2 Using markers and felt, decorate them to look like a snowman.

3 Glue the largest Styrofoam ball (the "bottom" of the snowman) to the underside of the jar's lid. Let dry.

4 Add pompom or mini foam-ball "flurries" and the other two Styrofoam balls to the jar.

5 Glue a ribbon to the lid and put it on the jar.

To Play

Start a timer. Begin shaking and moving the jar to build the snowman. Once the snowman is in order, stop the timer. See if you or someone else can beat your time.

Give a Gift of Gingerbread

Before You Begin Wash your hands.

Measure, mix, and share this recipe with someone special.

You Need

- ★ Index card
- ★ 1½ cups flour
- ★ ½ cup brown sugar
- ★ 1 teaspoon ground ginger
- ★ ¾ teaspoon cinnamon
- ★ ¾ teaspoon salt
- ★ ½ teaspoon ground cloves
- ★ ½ teaspoon baking powder
- ★ ½ teaspoon baking soda
- ★ ½ cup powdered sugar
- ★ Small plastic zip-top bag
- ★ 1-quart jar or plastic container with lid
- ★ Markers or crayons
- ★ Ribbon

 Yum!

Before You Begin

Adult: Write this recipe on a blank index card.

Gingerbread

Combine 1/3 cup oil, 1/3 cup mild molasses, 1/4 cup milk, and 1 beaten egg in a large mixing bowl. Open the jar, pull out the bag of powdered sugar, and set aside. Add the contents of the jar to the bowl. Mix until just combined. Pour into a greased 8-inch-by-4-inch-by-2-inch loaf pan. Bake at 350°F. for 30 minutes or until a toothpick inserted in the middle comes out clean. Cool completely.

To Make Glaze (optional): Combine powdered sugar with 1 tablespoon orange juice. Stir. Drizzle over cooled bread. Top with candied orange zest or candied orange peel, if desired.

Leave some blank space for decorating the card!

1 Measure the flour and pour it into a bowl. Measure the brown sugar and pour it into another bowl. Measure the ginger, cinnamon, salt, cloves, baking powder, and baking soda and pour into a third bowl.

2 Measure the powdered sugar and pour it into a small zip-top bag.

3 Put half of the flour into the jar or plastic container. Add the brown sugar. Then add the rest of the flour. Add the spices. Then add the zip-top bag and close the container.

4 Decorate the recipe card. Punch a hole in the card. Thread a ribbon through the hole and tie it around the container.

Pouch Present

You Need
* 9-inch-by-12-inch sheet of felt
* Scissors
* Markers
* Hole punch
* Yarn
* Paper clip

Before You Begin

Adult: Trace a large circle onto the felt. Cut it out. Draw 12 evenly spaced dots around the circle, 1/2 inch from the edge. Use a hole punch to make a hole in each dot. Tie a 36-inch length of yarn to a paper clip.

1 Decorate the felt with markers.

2 Push the paper clip through a hole on the circle. Pull most of the yarn through the hole, leaving a yarn "tail."

3 Keep "sewing" around the circle, going down through one hole and up through the next.

4 Stop when you reach the last hole. Now you have two yarn tails. Remove the paper clip from the yarn.

5 To close the pouch, pinch the felt between the first and last holes. Pull the yarn tails. Tie the yarn into a bow.

Answers

▼ Pages 2–3

▼ Page 4

▼ Pages 6–7

▼ Page 8

▼ Pages 10–11

▼ Pages 12–13

Answers

▼ **Pages 14–15**

▼ **Page 16**

▼ **Page 17**

▼ **Page 18**

▼ **Page 19**

Snowflakes
Striped Sleeves
Buttons

Snowflakes
Bows

Snowflakes
Same color
Turtlenecks

Zig-zags
Striped Sleeves

Zig-zags
Bows
Buttons
Turtlenecks

Zig-zags
Same color

Stripes
Striped Sleeves
Turtlenecks

Stripes
Bows

Stripes
Same Color
Buttons

▼ **Page 20**

▼ **Page 21**

▼ Pages 22–23

▼ Pages 26–27

▼ Page 28

▼ Pages 30–31

▼ Page 32

Answers

▼ Pages 34–35

▼ Pages 36–37

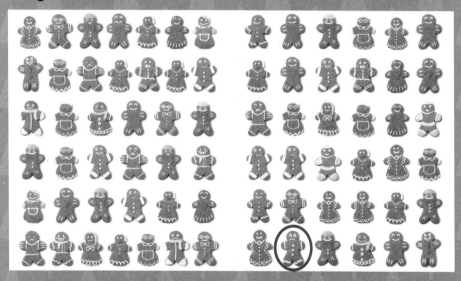

▼ Pages 38–39

▼ Page 40

▼ Page 41

▼ Page 42

Ice Rink Red Base Snowing | Ice Rink Arched Shape | Ice Rink Snowman Dog

Sled Red Base | Sled Arched Shape Snowing Dog | Sled Snowman

Pine Tree Red Base Dog | Pine Tree Arched Sahpe | Pine Tree Snowman Snowing

▼ Page 43

▼ Page 45

▼ Page 46

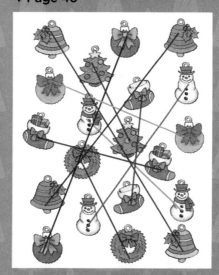

▼ Page 47

▼ Page 48

▼ Page 49

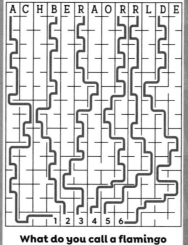

What do you call a flamingo at the North Pole? A BRRRD

Answers

▼ Pages 50–51

▼ Page 53

▼ Pages 54–55

▼ Page 56

▼ Page 57

▼ Pages 58–59

Answers

▼ Pages 60–61

▼ Pages 62–63

▼ Page 64

▼ Page 65

▼ Pages 66–67

▼ Page 69

Answers

▼ Page 70

▼ Page 71

1-D/B
2-R
3-C/C
4-D/D
5-P/V

▼ Pages 74–75

▼ Page 77

For information about permission to reprint selections from this book,
please contact permissions@highlights.com.
Published by Highlights Press
815 Church Street
Honesdale, Pennsylvania 18431
ISBN: 978-1-64472-841-3
Manufactured in Shenzhen, Guangdong, China
Mfg. 06/2023
First edition
Visit our website at Highlights.com.
10 9 8 7 6 5 4 3 2

Cover art by Mitch Mortimer
Craft photos by Guy Cali Associates, Inc., except door (page 83) by iStock/Liliboas and
gingerbread illustrations (pages 86–87) by Chuck Dillon.

JOY

SNOW

HOLLY

TO SANTA

MERRY

Highlights

MERRY & BRIGHT

MERRY CHRISTMAS

JOLLY

JOY

HOLLY

SNOW

Highlights